The God That I Know:

A JOURNEY
to
INTIMACY

TOMMY ALMONTE

**CREATION
HOUSE PRESS**
A STRANG COMPANY

THE GOD THAT I KNOW by Tommy Almonte
Published by Creation House Press
A Strang Company
600 Rinehart Road
Lake Mary, Florida 32746
www.creationhouse.com

Unless otherwise noted, Scripture quotations are from the Holy Bible, New International Version. Copyright © 1973, 1978, 1984, International Bible Society. Used by permission.

Cover design by Terry Clifton

Library of Congress Control Number: 2004114753

International Standard Book Number: 1-59185-719-8

04 05 06 07 08 — 987654321

Printed in the United States of America

Contents

I dedicate The God That I Know: A Journey to Intimacy *to you, Theresa, my lovely wife and closest friend. Thank you for your continuous encouragement and support in pursuing intimacy with God.*

Introduction

THE GOD THAT I Know: A Journey to Intimacy high-
lights a sequence of events in my life that led to the
pursuit of an intimate relationship with Jesus. As the
result of my curiosity to develop a relationship with God, this
book was written to reveal that spiritual journey toward intimacy with the Lord Jesus Christ. You will laugh and cry as
you read about the ups and downs of this journey. Without
question, the friendship that Jesus offered to me could only be
realized as I developed a relationship with the Holy Spirit.

In the Book of Genesis we read about Adam and Eve and
their relationship with God, who visited them daily and talked
with them in the cool of the day (Genesis 4:7–9). From Genesis to Revelation, the Bible describes God as a loving Father
who longs for an intimate relationship with people—all of us.

From the beginning of Creation, the Bible reveals just how
God intended to have a loving relationship with mankind; a

1

relationship one day broken as a result of Adam and Eve's disobedience to Him. Since that tragic day, God has worked to restore intimacy with mankind. I can only imagine how difficult it must have been for a loving Father who desires to fellowship with us to see us reject His love. But our rejection did not stop Him from pursuing us. Throughout the Old and New Testaments, God continued to communicate with mankind through His prophets, as well as through dreams and visions. Finally, His desire to be with us was so strong that he sent His only Son, Jesus Christ, to restore the relationship once lost. Through His death at Calvary, Jesus created a new bridge so we can once again fellowship with our Creator. Still, He does not violate the will of man; we must choose to enter into that fellowship through receiving salvation through faith in our Savior, Jesus Christ.

After I welcomed His invitation to enter into a personal relationship with Christ, I was not disappointed. I learned that Jesus would strategically guide my life. And all I needed to do was allow Him to connect all of my experiences, past and present, and bring out of them God's signature of love and commitment to fellowship with me. I invite you to join me as I relate my journey that led from my unbearable pain into a captivating love story, which could only be possible through the love of my Savior, Jesus Christ. This indescribably loving Savior has become the God that I know.

THE FORMAT

This book is divided into five chapters, representing five facets of my personal journey. Each chapter describes part of the process God used, through different life experiences, to bring me into relationship with Him.

In Chapter 1, I discuss lessons learned during my early years, many of which were reinforced in life by my parents who always reminded me of God's love and desire to communicate with us. Some of these early childhood experiences developed a curiosity within me to pursue a relationship with Jesus. Others, frankly, made me determined to avoid certain aspects of the church life I had experienced.

In Chapter 2, I share the painful process through which I walked that resulted in my reaching out to engage in a relationship with Jesus, experiencing new and unfamiliar territory as I pursued intimacy with Him.

Chapter 3 unfolds my surprising encounter with the Holy Spirit and the struggles I experienced as I came face to face with fears and misconceptions about this Third of the Trinity—God, the Holy Spirit.

In Chapter 4, I share how the Holy Spirit used various biblical accounts of people's lives to remove all of my fears and establish a strong foundation for developing a relationship with Jesus. These testimonies will encourage and strengthen your walk and friendship with Him.

Then, in Chapter 5, I share intimate moments I experienced with the Holy Spirit, which helped me to have a better understanding of Jesus. It is my hope that reading these experiences may also help you to have a better understanding of Jesus and that your life may be changed forever.

At the end of each chapter is a Bible Study Guide that will help the reader to understand and apply in greater detail the concepts discussed in that chapter. The Study Guide provides questions to help you evaluate your thinking as you continue to develop your relationship with Jesus.

I pray that this book will create within you a curiosity to know God, and specifically to know His Word—the Bible. I also pray that the Holy Spirit will become your best Friend. The first step to engaging in an intimate relationship with Jesus is to acknowledge the Holy Spirit as He is—a Person sent to guide us into intimacy with Jesus. Let us not allow our accomplishments and titles to keep us from approaching Him as a child. His attention can only be captured when we decide to place everything in the balance and listen for Him whisper our name. That surrender will be the beginning of an incredible journey, as the apostle Paul declared:

> We do, however, speak a message of wisdom among the mature, but not the wisdom of this age or the rulers of this age, who are coming to nothing. No, we speak of God's secret wisdom, a wisdom that has been hidden and that God destined for our glory before time began. None of the rulers of this age understood it, for if they had, they would not have crucified the Lord of glory. However, as it is written: "No eye has seen, no ear has heard, no mind has conceived what God has prepared for those who love him"—but God has revealed it to us by his Spirit. The Spirit searches all things, even the deep things of God. For who among men knows the thoughts of a man except the man's spirit within him? In the same way no one knows the thoughts of God except the Spirit of God. We have not received the spirit of the world but the Spirit who is from God, that we may understand what God has freely given us. This is what we speak, not in words taught us by human wisdom but in words taught by the Spirit, expressing spiritual truths in spiritual words. The man without the Spirit does not accept the things that come from the Spirit of God, for they are foolishness to him, and he cannot understand them, because they are spiritually discerned.
>
> —1 CORINTHIANS 2: 6–14

As you prepare to read about my personal journey, I hope you will follow the Study Guide designed to help you in your personal journey toward intimacy with God. Ask the Holy Spirit to reveal to you the things that God has hidden, His spiritual truths that those who seek intimacy with Him can discern.

The Holy Spirit is here to help you walk through unfamiliar territory as you pursue a deeper relationship with God the Father, God the Son, and God the Holy Spirit. Though the

Father, Son and Holy Spirit are referred to in the Scriptures by many names, my personal favorite is to call them Friends. It is that intimate relationship that God desires with each of His sons and daughters as we choose to know Him in that way.

Chapter 1

The Foundation
CHILDHOOD EXPERIENCES

ROBERT AND I spent most of our free time together. We became more than friends—we were family. In my opinion, we had the coolest bicycles of all the kids on our block. People in our neighborhood knew when we were coming because the loud noise from the red plastic cup attached to the back tire of our bikes created a rhythmic motorcycle hum. To make our fantasy more realistic, we enhanced our biker image with authentic motorcycle helmets and thick, dark shades.

Our homes were within walking distance of the ocean, so we spent most of our free time riding our bikes on the beach by the water, or pretending to be in a motorcycle race on the "professional race track" we built behind our homes. Sometimes we just spent time lying on the roof of our homes, watching the ocean and talking about life. Ours was a carefree, childhood friendship in a "pretend" world all our own.

FAMILY TIME

My parents were very busy people. My dad worked extremely hard as a salesman for a pharmaceutical company and my mom spent her days and nights ministering from one church to another. We attended the same church five days a week—or at least that is how it seemed to me. I remember falling asleep under the pew most of the time and, magically, waking up in my bed at home. The adults would pray for hours. A normal service gave my friends and me enough time to play, eat, and, in-between, catch a couple of refreshing catnaps.

During the services, we sang songs repeatedly, seemingly without end. Almost all of the songs were hymns. To this day, I remember some of the hymns we use to sing. One of my much-loved songs was:

> At the cross, at the cross where I first saw the light, and the burden of my heart rolled away. It was there by faith I received my sight, and now I am happy all the days; are you washed in the Blood of the Lamb? Are you fully trusting in Him? Are you washed in the Blood?[1]

We would always follow *At the Cross* by singing the following song:

> There is power, power, wonder-working power, in the blood of the lamb...[2]

I cannot really say I fully understood at the time what I was singing, but I sure loved those old hymns! After each service, we always visited the house of one of the members, whether for a meal, to pray for the sick, or to give a ride home to some of the church members. Our 1968 light brown Renault was

---

[1] Issac Watts, *At the Cross*. Public Domain.
[2] Lewis Edgar Jones, *There Is Power in the Blood*. Public Domain.

the unofficial bus for our small church and the designated bus driver was—none other than my dad.

PRAYER

Prayer, fasting, and reading of the Bible were three very important biblical practices in our home. My parents believed in the power and protection that resulted from these disciplines. Every morning, my three siblings and I were expected to gather in my parent's room to pray together as a family.

This devotional routine even included weekends. I really did not mind the weekly tradition, but found the weekend devotionals to be a true burden. Sometimes my parents made my friends wait outside until everyone was up and ready to pray as a family. On some occasions, my friends were so tired of waiting for me that they would come in and join us as we prayed. My parents had a "no exceptions to the rule" policy.

FASTING

It was customary in our home for my parents to call a family meeting about once a month. I remember, during one meeting in particular, my parents educated us on a subject that turned into a gruesome task during my childhood years. At the time they were giving us the lesson, I was oblivious to the true intentions of their education on such a subject. Much to my horror, I would soon discover this truth for myself.

They wanted my siblings and me to know that we were old enough to understand the biblical meaning of fasting. They gave us a history from the Bible of how fasting made a big difference in peoples' lives, declaring that an entire city was even saved because of the act of fasting (see the Book of Jonah). We did not know where they were going with this lesson, but were fascinated with the stories, so we listened intently. Much to our chagrin, their presentation ended with an idea that would

9

change our lives forever. My parents decided that, as a family, we were going to fast one Saturday of every month. We still did not really grasp the significance of this decision until the word *food* was mentioned. After that, no further explanation of fasting was needed.

I considered this decision to be detrimental to my health. "What?...No food?!" was my response. We were expected not to eat for an entire day. And that was not the extent of my parents' decision. Their final, death-defying blow was their declaration that there would be no extra-curricular activities outside of the home on the monthly day of fasting.

This was too much for a small, tender child to handle! "Wait a minute," was my next response. But by the end of our family meeting, the decision determined: there would be no food and no friends one Saturday of every month. Thanks to our bargaining abilities, or possibly the mercy of my parents, they relented and cut our fasting time to a half a day.

My mind was always flowing with new creative ideas and inventions, so to speak. "Oh yes! I could make it until noon," I had thought to myself, "I have a creative solution." It was very simple. My plan was to eat as much food as I could the night before and to sleep in as late as I could the following day. I felt like I had once again fooled the wise old folks. A true genius child, I was. The tables had turned in my favor, and I felt very much in control of the situation. Like strategists, planning out their final attack on the enemy, I had everything perfectly planned.

However, there was an inkling of a problem in my plan. It was a shortfall to my strategy that I had not foreseen. After consuming massive amounts of food the day before our fast day, I would still just "happen" to wake up early that Saturday morning—and feel as hungry as ever. Those four to five hours of fasting seemed to my child's mind like days without end—almost eternal. Food never tasted so good every time I finished my half-day fast.

Family Meetings

My first encounter with the Holy Spirit happened at the early age of nine. It was during the summer of 1982. One night I had a dream. I dreamed I was in the living room playing and a gentle Voice started speaking to me. The Voice proceeded to share with me very specific details concerning each family member in our home. When I woke up the following day, I remembered the dream but did not think much of it.

However, throughout the day, the conversation I had with this Voice kept replaying in my head. I was not able to concentrate as I played with my green soldiers. But I still thought that it was just one of those dreams that would eventually go away.

The following night I had the same dream again. This time the Person talking to me reminded me not to be afraid. He told me He was God. And He said I was to share these "specific things" with the rest of the family. I remember waking up and thinking to myself, "What is going on here?"

I went to my mom and explained the reoccurring dream to her; I began to share with her what God had said to me. She took a moment to explain that sometimes God speaks to people. My mom reassured me and said I should not be scared. She also said it was time to call a family meeting.

As you can imagine, just the thought of calling a family meeting to announce that God had talked to me and told me to tell them what He said was nerve-wracking, to say the least. The day for the family meeting came; none of my siblings knew what was about to happen. I sure did not want to stand in front of everyone and start my sentence with, "God talked to me," but I was committed to putting this whole thing behind me, and I knew the only way to do that was by sharing with everyone what I needed to say.

My dad finished giving his normal updates, concerns, and expectations, and then the stage was mine. I remember suddenly feeling an overwhelming presence of the Holy Spirit in our room. I felt energized and confident to share. Our time together went better than I had expected. The content of what I shared pertained to current as well as prophetic events affecting our family. The end of that family meeting was the beginning of many positive changes in my life and in our home.

THE LOSS OF A FRIEND

Robert and I had lost contact for a number of years due to our family moving from our native country, the Dominican Republic, to Michigan. Years later, after the family move, we reconnected and became even closer friends. Robert and his family relocated to New York, which was good news for the future relationship of old friends. Our friendship grew with renewed contact and as we confided in each other the challenges and struggles of being young adults.

One winter day, as I walked through the doors of my house to find relief from a brutal cold, I was welcomed with a quiet hello from my mom. It was obvious that something very bad had happened. Before I had a chance to ask her what was wrong, she uttered the following devastating words: "Robert is dead."

I cannot explain the state of mind in that moment. I just know that the word *pain* cannot even begin to describe what I felt after receiving this news. All I could ask was the how, when, and the why of it all. I wanted to know everything in a matter of seconds. After the initial shock, my mother explained what really happened. I was not prepared for what she was about to share.

"Robert committed suicide," my mom quietly informed me.

I bowed my head in disbelief and desperation as my mind, soul, and spirit seemed instantly paralyzed, unable to comprehend this horror.

"Why? Why? Why?" I repeatedly stammered as hot tears streamed down my face. Later that night, as I sorrowfully wept on the phone with Robert's mom, she described how his frozen body was found sitting on the corner of their patio.

"My God, my God! Why?" was the only thing I could moan.

The bad news did not end there. My plans to see him and say my farewell for the last time were frustrated, proving to be impossible. With every second that passed, the chance to say my final goodbye diminished. Due to the distance and the short notice, by the time I would have arrived, his body would have found its final resting place in the Dominican Republic. I was overwhelmed with the incomprehensible reality that the body of my best friend was en route to our native land in the cargo area of a plane. Once again we were separated—but this time with no chance to reunite.

Study Guide

Scriptures for Meditation
Proverbs 22:6
Deuteronomy 6:5–9; 11:18–20
Acts 16:31–34

Summary Statements

- Our relationship with the Holy Spirit is reflected in our homes.

- The standards and principles we support in our homes are the foundation of our future as well as our children's future.

- God's promises to our families described in Proverbs 22:6 are for you and me.

Questions to Consider

1. What principles are you living and teaching in your home? Describe.

2. Does the dynamic with your family or friends reflect the relationship Jesus wants us to have with Him?

3. Are God's promises evident in your life?

4. Does the promise of God described in Proverbs 22:6 apply to your family and friends?

5. Take a moment to reflect on ways that your home can be a display of the principles of God.

Chapter 2

Reaching Out

WHO IS THIS GOD?

URING THE YEARS following the death of Robert, I
made it a point not to associate with anything that
represented God. I intentionally became occupied
with life and walked as far away as I could from the church
and everything that it represented. I knew how to accomplish
that goal, and college was the perfect place to hide. I made
a handful of friends who, in their own ways, encouraged my
"new" way of life.

On one of my trips with a friend, we decided to visit a
well-known, five-star prostitution house. From the recom-
mendation of other people in the area, this was the place to
go if you were willing to pay for it. I was very uncomfortable with the idea, as I knew that this decision was going to
open a whole new world to me. I guess my conscience was
still alive, but my anger toward God was so strong that I still
agreed to the decision.

We finally arrived at "the place", a beautiful half million-dollar home in the middle of nowhere. As we were walking toward the entrance, my forehead ran into what felt like the hand of Someone pushing me back a couple of steps. With a concerned look on his face, my friend asked me if I was all right.

I looked around stunned. "You go ahead," was my shaken reply as I walked toward the car. I was trying to make sense of what had just happened. The thought of that hand pressing on my forehead gave me a lot to think about while I waited for my friend in the car.

TIME TO DECIDE

Such was the impact of that "hand" on my mind that I spent many days and nights thinking about that incident. I felt as if there were an imprint of the hand still on my forehead. I was torn inside between following my own rebellious decisions and goals and surrendering myself to a relationship with a God I really did not know and wasn't sure I wanted to. I was full of questions with no apparent answers on the horizon.

There was no happiness within me as I tried to adapt to the sinful ways of the world. I had no peace; the pleasure this world offered me made me feel more and more empty. I did not want go back to the church because I was equally unhappy there. I found myself stuck between two worlds. On one hand, I never felt fulfilled while perusing my own desires; on the other, I felt like the church had nothing to offer me. I needed to find a way out of my misery.

One night as I contemplated my past, present, and possible future relationship with God, I decided on a plan that would give God one last chance. I was going to pursue Him with all my might, and if I could not find Him, then, I would have the right to walk away from God and everything He represented. I told God if I could not find Him, He had no right to bother me in my personal pursuit of happiness. I felt like we shook hands on the deal that night and made an agreement. I was really hoping not to find Him. I just wanted to find a way out of this miserable place of indecision between two worlds!

THE PURSUIT

During my childhood years, growing up in the church, I was exposed to the Holy Spirit, but I really did not know Him. I realized that my introduction to the things of God from early childhood and the knowledge imparted by my parents created a connection between the Holy Spirit and me. Being far from Him made me feel uncomfortable, but at the same time I never felt at peace while in the church. I became tired of pretending that I was satisfied at church.

The decision was made. I agreed to pursue a relationship with Jesus, but I wanted to know if there was more to it than just attending church. In my struggle, it felt as though two different worlds were fighting within me. I wanted a personal relationship with Jesus, but I also wanted to be free to come and go without being reminded of my sins by the Holy Spirit.

On the first day of my journey after my decision to pursue God, my plan was simple. It was to start living life in a fresh way. I was going to remove all the preconception and expectations I had about God and try to approach Him with an open mind and heart. I took a Bible, and started reading Genesis, chapter one. I did not know what to expect; I just knew that, because of my decision, this was it. There was no turning back. I was committed to finding answers. I wanted to know if a "typical Joe" like me could really have a committed relationship with Jesus.

God speaks to those who listen.

THE LIGHT CAME ON

After reading halfway through the Book of Genesis, I began to understand the meaning of two key concepts that would begin to change my whole life: *relationship* and *intimacy.* The realization that my dissatisfaction with God and life might really be a lack of an intimate relationship with Jesus changed the focus of my search for God. Curiosity welled up within me.

Was it possible to enjoy intimacy with God? If so, then how? My mind was full of questions as I entertained these new concepts I had never considered before. I could not wait to continue reading the Bible to find the answer to my questions.

INTIMACY WITH GOD? WHAT A CONCEPT!

A key account in the Book of Genesis became the focal point of my pursuit of God, and later proved to become the impetus to my relationship with Him. In Genesis 15, there is a fascinating account that reflects an intimate relationship between God and a mortal being. In my opinion, their relationship reached one of the deepest levels of intimacy known to men.

According to the biblical account, God made a promise to a person named Abram. He was advanced in age and had no offspring, no children with whom he could leave his wealth. As he contemplated his life, he became concerned about the future. As in today's society, at the moment of Abram's death, strangers would devour all the wealth he had accumulated. Abram prayed continually to God for a son. God understood his pain and made him a promise. God promised Abram that he would have a son before his spirit departed from this earth.

During one of Abram's encounters with the living God, God changed his name from Abram to Abraham to reflect the impact of their divine relationship. Then in Genesis 18, the Bible records that three men visited Abraham. The story does not go into detail as to who two of the three visitors were, but many Bible scholars concur that one of them was a pre-incarnate appearance of the Lord. The account goes on to describe their encounter with Abraham and explain the reason for their visitation. The Lord came in person to fulfill the promise He had made to Abraham and Sarah, his wife.

THE ESSENCE OF OUR RELATIONSHIP

As the biblical account continues, the Lord shared the wonderful news with Abraham and Sarah that by the following year at that time they would have a son, though they were both past the age of childbearing. Shortly after the news was given, the three visitors prepared to leave. Abraham accompanied them part of the way. It was then that the Lord asked a question that, when I read it, impacted me in such a way that it would form the core of my relationship with God:

> When the men got up to leave, they looked down toward Sodom, and Abraham walked along with them to see them on their way. Then the Lord said, "Shall I hide from Abraham what I am about to do?
> —GENESIS 18:16–17

As I continued to read this account of Abraham's amazing relationship with the Lord, it became clear to me that the foundation of their relationship could only be described in one word—*intimacy*. It was that intimacy that required the Lord to ask that startling question and, ultimately, to share His heart with Abraham.

I was blown away to see that the God who created the heavens and the earth, who gave life to every human being, and who holds the key of death and life in His hands, would follow the same guidelines as you and I do in cultivating relationship. God was not forced to share His heart with Abraham, but He understood the value of sharing openly once intimacy characterizes a relationship. He wanted us to know that He is willing to follow the same guidelines we do in relationship.

What a thought! Here we see Jesus torn between sharing information that would give a human being the ability to affect His plans, following the same principle that applies to you and me in a relationship. I can picture the Lord turning around to the other two men with a serious look on his face as He asks, "Should I do this? What do you two think?"

The realization I came to that day, that God not only encourages us to share openly in relationship, respecting the intimacy that has been created, but that He Himself respects and follows that same principle in relationship, was amazing to me. His example in this account of such intimacy in relationship with God has become my obsession; it is at the center of my relationship with God. Realizing His approach to intimacy in His relationship with Abraham gave me the freedom to become vulnerable in my pursuit of intimacy with Him. I understood that He would also bare His heart to me.

I have come to understand that the pursuit of intimacy in any relationship is as vital to the relationship as water or oxygen is to our bodies. The desire for intimacy and the pursuit of it keeps a relationship alive. As more time passes, intimacy in a relationship becomes the roadmap to a long and happy friendship—and life. King David said it best when talking about intimacy with the Lord.

> The LORD confides in those who fear him; he makes his covenant known to them.
>
> —PSALM 25:14

WHAT'S NEXT?

At that point, all I knew was that intimacy with Jesus was what I wanted. But I did not know how or where to start cultivating the intimacy I had recognized between Abraham and the Lord. I was encouraged by the realization that an intimate relationship with Jesus was attainable. But at the same time, I felt discouraged as I found no answer to some basic questions: Where do I start? What is the process?

I felt like a person who discovered a mine of gold but had no knowledge of how to extract it. I knelt in my room that day and asked Jesus to show me the way to reach His heart. I did not get any big revelations, but instead began to be filled with an inexplicable hunger to read the Bible. And in that reading, I found the answers to all of my questions.

ROAD MAP TO INTIMACY

As I continued to read the Bible, I found another important piece to this puzzle in the Book of Exodus. I learned about the life of Moses, a person who at a young age reached high levels of success. Later in life, he found himself at his lowest point of defeat, and that is where he met God. Moses understood that there was more to life than just getting up in the morning and handling the activities of the day. He understood we were created to develop an intimate relationship with our Creator.

Moses acknowledged that he needed to know God. He declared: "If you are pleased with me, teach me your ways so I may know you and continue to find favor with you" (Exod. 33:13). Moses realized that the only way to know God was to know His ways. I started to connect the dots and discovered that in order to engage in an intimate relationship with Jesus, I needed to learn His ways.

GOD'S WAYS

Everything God created involves a process and protocol that must be followed. Our inability to understand and follow the required protocol would exclude us from having an intimate relationship with God.

In the Book of Deuteronomy, we find a set of protocols, or as Moses described them, "God's ways," for enjoying an intimate relationship with Jesus. Moses explained to the nation of Israel the ways of God in the wilderness:

> He humbled you, causing you to hunger and then feed-
> ing you with manna, which neither you nor your fathers

21

had known, to teach you that man does not live on bread alone but on every word that comes from the mouth of the LORD.

—DEUTERONOMY 8:3

I must say that God's protocol, according to Moses, for having an intimate relationship with Him was not what I was expecting. My expectation might have been more like: "In the middle of the night a light will enter into your room and a voice will reveal to you all you need to know about His ways."

But I kept playing over in my mind the process Moses described in Deuteronomy 8:3: first, God is going to humble me; then He is going to allow me to be hungry; then He is going to feed me supernaturally. After that, I will know God in a way that neither my father nor I had known. I thought to myself, *that sounds like at lot of work. Who in their right mind is going to stick around to see that happen?* But then in the same breath I thought, *I really want an intimate relationship with Him.*

THE HOLY SPIRIT: WHAT A FRIEND!

From reading the Book of Genesis, I understood that the Holy Spirit played an important role in our protocol for developing an intimate relationship with Jesus. The Bible speaks of Him as the Person sent by Jesus to guide us into His presence.

The Holy Spirit as my guide between Jesus and me created a problem for me. My perception of the Holy Spirit was not very good. From growing up in the church, I had negative experiences of watching people who were supposedly "guided" or "led" by the Holy Spirit; I did not want to be associated with the Holy Spirit if that was how I had to act. I saw people who proclaimed to be guided by the Holy Spirit and were rejected by the church due to their psychotic behaviors. I did not want to play around with this type of "force" or "spirit." I guess my childhood fears and lack of knowledge were the basis for my view of who the Holy Spirit was.

From reading the Scriptures, I realized that in order to develop an intimate relationship with Jesus, I needed to reevaluate my perception of the Holy Spirit. Even though I had some hesitation, I decided to start all over and put all the bad memories related to my concept of the Holy Spirit aside.

As I studied through the pages of the Bible, a new image of the Holy Spirit began to appear. My perception of Him changed from thinking of Him as a "ghost" to recognizing Him as a Person, like you and me, with feelings and emotions. Though He is God, the Third Person of the Trinity, the Book of Ephesians helped me to understand that the Holy Spirit is capable of getting hurt and feeling rejected:

> And do not grieve the Holy Spirit of God, with whom you were sealed for the day of redemption.
> —EPHESIANS 4:30

It amazed me to think that I could grieve the Holy Spirit. I remember feeling overwhelmed by the realization that my behavior had hurt the Holy Spirit. In my mind's eye, a big TV screen opened up allowing me to see the many instances when I laughed at and mocked the Holy Spirit. Now I realized it was time to develop a reverent, loving relationship with the Holy Spirit.

MORE PROTOCOL

The Scriptures showed me that in order for the Holy Spirit and me to develop a good relationship, several steps needed to take place. I understood that the omission of any of these steps would lead to an empty and unfulfilling relationship, and I could not afford to play games. I was grasping the realization that intimacy to a relationship is like fuel to an engine—without intimacy a relationship has no power, no life.

If I wanted to develop an intimate relationship with the Holy Spirit, my perception of Him needed to change. I needed to acknowledge that my behavior and attitude towards the Holy Spirit was offensive and causing hurt in His life. I expected the Holy Spirit to have the same expectations of Jesus in a relationship. And I thought about the protocol we follow as we develop a human relationship. First, we introduce ourselves. If necessary, we apologize or ask for forgiveness for past behaviors. Next, we are reconciled and then begin to spend quality time together.

For the first time I also understood that, just as intimacy did not occur in a group setting in human relationships, so it would occur as I spent time alone with the Holy Spirit. There was only one thing left to do—I must address the Holy Spirit as He is and ask for forgiveness for my past behavior toward Him.

I went to my room, closed the door, and proceeded with a "proper" introduction to the Holy Spirit. I realized that my whole body was shaking. Perhaps it was because I was about to face my past.

I started my introduction by saying in a raspy, quiet voice; "Holy Spirit, I am feeling very uncomfortable talking to You. I can't see You, but I know You are here. I have been learning about You in the Word of God, and I know you are a Person with feelings and emotions, not the 'ghost' I pictured you to be. Please forgive me for all the times I hurt You; I was so afraid of You and did not want to be associated with You. But I now realize You are a Person and that You are here. Please forgive me; I want to be Your friend. Welcome to my home; You are welcome in this room and in my life."

There was no loud voice or smoke in my room, but I felt such a profound sense of relief and such deep forgiveness that it could only have come from Him.

Following the protocol in a relationship is the first step to intimacy.

HE SPOKE MY NAME

The following morning, after my introduction to the Holy Spirit, I got up early to pray. I set a goal to schedule quality time in the morning with the Holy Spirit. As I walked into the room, I was greeted by a soft voice: "Good morning, Tommy."

Without thinking, I replied, "Good morning!"

Then I thought to myself, *What has just happened?* Was I talking to myself? I did not mention this experience to anyone for fear I would be identified as being a good candidate for "psychiatric treatment."

The following morning, when I walked into my room, the same thing happened. And once again, I answered, "Good morning," and went on to spend time with the Holy Spirit. That was the beginning of a long and intimate relationship with the Holy Spirit. After several years of meeting with Him every morning, I still love to hear Him say my name.

NO CONDEMNATION IN HIM

From growing up in church, I had my own definition of God. I did not think of Him as a loving, caring God who desires to know us on a personal level and is ready to forgive our wrongdoings, but instead I thought of Him as an old man who watches everything you do and keeps a record of your sins and mistakes to use against you when required. My definition of God led to many wrong expectations of Him.

In the beginning of my new relationship with the Holy Spirit, I found myself restrained by these expectations that I placed on the relationship. It wasn't long before I realized that most of my decisions were not motivated by love for the Holy Spirit, but were driven by my own outlook, which in time led to condemnation. Yet I read in the Scriptures:

Therefore, there is now no condemnation for those who are in Christ Jesus.

—ROMANS 8:1

During my time with the Holy Spirit, He reminded me of the story in the Bible found in the Book of John:

The teachers of the law and the Pharisees brought in a woman caught in adultery. They made her stand before the group and said to Jesus, "Teacher, this woman was caught in the act of adultery. In the Law Moses commanded us to stone such women. Now what do you say?" They were using this question as a trap, in order to have a basis for accusing him. But Jesus bent down and started to write on the ground with his finger. When they kept on questioning him, he straightened up and said to them, "If any one of you is without sin, let him be the first to throw a stone at her." Again he stooped down and wrote on the ground. At this, those who heard began to go away one at a time, the older ones first, until Jesus was left, with the woman still standing there. Jesus straightened up and asked her, "Woman, where are they? Has no one condemned you?" "No one, sir," she said. "Then neither do I condemn you," Jesus declared, "Go now and leave your life of sin."

—JOHN 8:3–11

This story describes a sinful woman whom Jesus encountered. The woman was caught in the act of adultery. The teachers of the law and Pharisees brought her to Jesus to see how He was going to deal with her. They expected Jesus to respond in a certain way. The proper response during that time was to follow the Law of Moses. The penalty for a person committing adultery was to be stoned to death. The Bible says the teachers and Pharisees were trying to trap Jesus. They wanted to see if He was going to support the Law given to Moses by His Father or if He was going to side with the sinful woman, apparently rejecting the Law.

Jesus knew the Law and He was aware of the punishment expected for such crimes. But He could not meet their expectations because within Him there was, and still is, no condemnation. In other words, Jesus was unable to condemn the woman by the Law based upon her actions. I realized that I had entered into a friendship with a Person who is unable to condemn me, even if our society would require it. Understanding this principle of divine mercy has given me the freedom to follow Jesus with all of my imperfections.

HIS EXPECTATION

In the beginning of my pursuit of intimacy with the Holy Spirit, I became discouraged. I found myself falling into a deep sleep every time I met with Him. After trying different techniques to stay awake and not succeeding, I became frustrated. The process that I thought would get me closer to the Holy Spirit seemed, in fact, to be pushing me further away from Him. I felt so ashamed that I did not look forward to spending time with Him. I felt like I was letting Him down.

One morning I walked into my prayer room discouraged and with a heavy cloud of guilt hanging over my head because I continued to fall asleep when seeking Him. I must have looked like a cow being led to the slaughter. That morning the Lord spoke to my spirit; what He said changed my whole perspective. In a quiet way, the Holy Spirit let me know that He only expected me to show up and He would do the rest. Once again, I realized that my ideas of our relationship were not in line with His.

The Holy Spirit used a short verse found in the Book of Genesis to remind me of what he expected of me during our time together. "The Lord God caused the man to fall into a deep sleep; and while he was sleeping, he took one of the man's ribs and closed up the place with flesh" (Gen. 2:21). He reminded me that while Adam was sleeping, God was creating life out of him. He taught me that sometimes God's best work is done while we sleep.

However, I must remind you that communication is vital to the health of an intimate relationship. Relationships have different stages. In my case, falling asleep in His presence only lasted a short period of time. Subsequently, this lead into another stage of reading His Word and conversing with God while in His presence.

The more intimate the Holy Spirit and I became, the more I realized that most of my expectations were not matching His expectations. I expected that the Holy Spirit was coming to spend time with me every morning with a long checklist of things that I needed to change in order to be His friend, when in reality the Holy Spirit just expected me to show up and spend time with Him.

STUDY GUIDE

SCRIPTURES FOR MEDITATION
2 Corinthians 12:10
Romans 8:26–28
Proverbs 16:9
Colossians 3:23
Jeremiah 29:13

SUMMARY STATEMENTS

- The Holy Spirit is our guide to help us walk in intimacy with Jesus.
- All our life experiences (good and bad) have a purpose in God's perfect plan for our lives.
- Our level of investment in our relationship with the Lord will determine the depth of our intimacy.
- God speaks to those who are willing to listen.
- God's way described in His Word is a road map to developing an intimate relationship with Jesus.
- Our weaknesses in God's hands become our foundation to a successful and fruitful life.

QUESTIONS TO CONSIDER

1. Who is God to you?

2. Describe your relationship with Jesus.

3. Have you given God permission to capture your whole heart?

4. Describe God's expectations of you as described in this chapter, and what are your expectations of God?

5. Does God have the ability to turn our weaknesses and failures into a source of support and strength? Read 2 Corinthians 12:7–10.

Chapter 3

The Best Jesus Had

THE HOLY SPIRIT

E VERYDAY I LEARN something new about the Holy Spirit in my walk with my Master and Savior, Jesus Christ. As I search for the Holy Spirit, the reality of Jesus becomes more clear and attainable to me. I am convinced that seeking relationship with the Holy Spirit is the only way to know Jesus. Jesus Himself declared:

> But when He, the Spirit of truth, comes, he will guide you into all truth. He will not speak on his own; He will speak only what He hears, and He will tell you what is yet to come. He will bring glory to me by taking from what is mine and making it known to you. All that belongs to the Father is mine. That is why I said the Spirit will take from what is mine and make it known to you.
> —JOHN 16: 13–15

WHO IS THE HOLY SPIRIT?

There are two requirements for developing a relationship with another person. First, we need to recognize the person for who they are; second, we need to accept them. Failing to meet these requirements can create a lack of intimacy in a relationship. The Bible gives us a clear picture of who the Holy Spirit is and what His role is. God's Word says that the Holy Spirit is a Person and that His role is to guide us into all truth. In order to experience all that God has for our family and ourselves we need to know the Holy Spirit.

I am so glad He is patient with us.

HE IS A PERSON WITH A PERSONALITY

As I initiated a relationship with the Holy Spirit, the concept that He is a Person was one of the most difficult concepts for me to accept. Up to this point in my life I thought the Holy Spirit was a "thing," without feelings, a divine entity floating out in the air. It took me a long time to really believe what the Bible says about Him and to address the Holy Spirit as a Person.

The more I read through the Bible the more I realized that the Holy Spirit is a divine Person—the Third Person of the Trinity. The Bible describes these three specific points, among others, that define the Holy Spirit as a Person:

Point one

As we have mentioned, in the Book of Ephesians the Holy Spirit is described as having emotions and being capable of having feelings:

> And do not grieve the Holy Spirit of God, with whom you were sealed for the day of redemption
> —EPHESIANS 4:30

Point two

In the apostle Paul's letter to the Corinthians, he explains another important aspect of the Holy Spirit—his ability to make decisions and having a will:

> All these are the works of one and the same Spirit, and he gives them (gifts) to each one, just as he determines.
> —1 CORINTHIANS 12:11

Point three

The Book of Romans describes another key to the Holy Spirit's personality; He is capable of knowing us intimately:

> And He who searches our hearts knows the mind of the Spirit, because the Spirit intercedes for the saints, in accordance with God's will.
> —ROMANS 8:27

From my prior understanding of what constitutes a personality, after discovering the truth of these three personality qualities of the Holy Spirit, I had no excuse to dismiss the reality that the Holy Spirit is a divine Person. I had two options: to accept the Bible's description of the Holy Spirit or to simply reject it and embrace my faulty definition of Him. I remember being afraid of becoming one of those "crazy" people that I had encountered at church during my childhood years.

Our curiosity to develop intimacy with the Holy Spirit must be stronger than our fears to change.

HIS ROLE

Recently my wife and I were invited to an event in a town about forty-five minutes away from our home. We arrived there with the help of a map we printed from an internet site. The map gave us the confidence we needed to jump into our red 1995 Chevy Blazer and head out to the event without any worries or concerns of getting lost. I thought to myself, *I have all I need to make it; I have a map and my wife as a co-pilot.*

Later that evening as the event came to a conclusion and we prepared to go home, we forgot to revisit the map. That was a bad decision. Disoriented, like a person who was waking up in an unfamiliar setting, we got into our vehicle and headed toward nowhere. After driving for about twenty minutes, searching for any sign of something that looked familiar to guide me, I admitted to my co-pilot that I was lost. I turned to my wife and said, " I hope you know where we are." She looked at me with a taunting face that said, You're the one driving. I slowed down while trying to decide whether to go back to the place where we had started or to find our way out of that place.

Another bad decision—we kept driving. We drove for another twenty minutes, looking desperately for anything that could lead us in the right direction. Thank God, we saw something familiar; we reached a small town that my wife recognized. "We are going the wrong way," she stated. After circling the area several times, we finally found our way home.

In the Book of John we read about the Holy Spirit and His work in the earth: "But when he, the Spirit of truth, comes, he will *guide* you into all truth. He will not speak on his own; he will speak only what he hears, and he will tell you what is yet to come" (John 16:13; emphasis mine).

The Holy Spirit is our guide. He is the only way to find Jesus. The Holy Spirit is the guide who leads us to Jesus.

OUR RELATIONSHIP

The Holy Spirit and I are starting to develop a meaningful relationship. I am feeling more comfortable addressing him as a Person. I still feel slightly uncomfortable with the idea that I can talk with Him; but giving Him His place has allowed me to approach our relationship as any other relationship with another Person. I have learned that intimacy with the Holy Spirit comes by getting to know Him over time. The secret places of the heart are revealed by the Spirit as the relationship deepens.

Intimacy takes time and does not take place in a group setting.

MOMENTS OF DOUBT IN HIS PRESENCE

Up to this point, I have not verbally questioned His presence, but in my mind I still questioned many things about the Holy Spirit. I have not fully overcome my amazement over the reality that the Holy Spirit is in my room and He loves to spend time with me. Sometimes I find myself torn, as my spirit is eager to be with Him, while my mind questions His presence.

One day, after spending some time with the Holy Spirit, reading a couple of chapters of the Bible and listening to a few songs, I went to sleep. I was awakened by the overwhelming feeling that Someone was in the room. As I opened my eyes, I saw in front of me a man about nine feet tall. His hair and body were the color of gold. He had a big belt around His waist. He had this elegant figure. This man looked at me and smiled. He did not identify Himself, but I knew He was the Holy Spirit. He stood there for about a minute and then, as if vapor, He walked away. For a few seconds, I tried to convince myself I was sleeping but as I looked to my left I could see my wife sleeping next to me. I was overwhelmed by the realization that He is a Person. I woke my wife up and asked her, "Did you see that?"

Half asleep she replied, "What?"

"Never mind, I'll tell you later." And with that she went back to sleep. I lay on my bed for about an hour. I could not wait to talk to Him the next day.

THE REQUIREMENTS OF INTIMACY

My wife and I have been married for over five years. She is my best friend. Everyday we give our relationship an opportunity to grow and increase in intimacy. Her honesty and complete trust in me is a reflection of our intimacy.

As we enter into a deeper level of intimacy in our marriage, the expectation to protect what is disclosed increases. We each expect the other to guard what is shared within the intimate boundaries of our marriage. An inability to understand such a concept would act like a death-blow to the growth and survival of our relationship. Our responsibility is to protect and guard the intimacy just as a person would guard precious stones.

The morning after being visited by the Holy Spirit, I could not stand still. Everything within me wanted to share with everyone what took place with the Holy Spirit. It just made sense. Something great had happened and it needed to be shared. I shared my experience with a few people, and the response received was not necessarily what I was expecting; the look in their faces was more of concern than excitement with my experience. I felt disappointed.

That night, with the help of the Holy Spirit, I came to realize that my desire to disclose this intimate experience with Him had placed my relationship at risk. As I walked into my prayer room, the first thing He said to me was, "Do not take my intimacy lightly; if you do I will leave." What a shocking moment!

I understood that this was not a game and that I had betrayed the intimacy He had offered to me. Tears flowed down my face and in a quiet voice I whispered, "Forgive me for betraying our intimacy."

He gently replied, "I forgive you."

Intimacy can only be shared with others when permission has been granted.

STUDY GUIDE

SCRIPTURES FOR MEDITATION
Acts 2:38, 39
John 14:16, 26; 16:13–15
1 Corinthians 12:1–11

SUMMARY STATEMENTS

- The Holy Spirit is the only way to know Jesus.

- The Holy Spirit is a divine Person with feelings and emotions.

- The Holy Spirit will guide us into all truth.

- Our ability to be a successful and fruitful person lies in our realization of who the Holy Spirit is and what His role is.

QUESTIONS TO CONSIDER

1. Who is the Holy Spirit to you?

2. Describe your relationship with the Holy Spirit.

3. List areas in your life that could potentially grieve the Holy Spirit.

4. What steps are you willing to take to change those areas?

5. According to the Book of John, can a person have an intimate relationship with Jesus without the Holy Spirit? Read John 16:12–15.

Chapter 4

Teaching Moments

GOD MOVES

THE MORE INTIMATELY I get to know the Holy Spirit the more I realize that God cannot be manipulated, but He acts in response to our desires by answering what is in our hearts as we align with His will.

My relationship with the Holy Spirit is now at a very comfortable level. We are becoming good friends. He always greets me as I walk into the room to spend time with Him, and our conversation and discussions are more open and nourishing.

I have noticed that my desire to talk with the Holy Spirit and be with Him was met daily. And as my relationship with Him grew, my desire for relationship with God also increased. He has always been faithful to reward my desire by visiting me during my devotional time.

The Holy Spirit and I have talked about how God can meet the desires of our heart. He gave me insight into several accounts from the Bible where God responded to the desire of men and women in the Bible.

In the Book of Acts, there is an account of a person who had a need and who confronted Peter and John with his need (Acts, chapter 3). The Bible records that Peter and John were going to the temple to pray when they encountered a crippled man who sat by the entrance of the temple to beg for money from those entering the temple:

> One day Peter and John were going up to the temple at the time of prayer—at three in the afternoon. Now a man crippled from birth was being carried to the temple gate called Beautiful, where he was put every day to beg from those going into the temple courts. When he saw Peter and John about to enter, he asked them for money. Peter looked straight at him, as did John. Then Peter said, "Look at us!" So the man gave them his attention, expecting to get something from them.
>
> —ACTS 3:1–5

The Holy Spirit pointed out to me from this biblical account several factors involved in developing healthy desires that we can take to the bank with God.

First:

Our desires should be based on the Word of the living God.

Second:

Our desires should be the result of our relationship with the Holy Spirit.

Third:

Our desires should be the offspring of our faith in God's abilities.

He reminded me that God intended for us to have desires and to receive accordingly. But these desires should only be the reflection of our relationship with Jesus and our daily walk with the Holy Spirit. Not until we know Jesus' character and personality can we form realistic desires that will always bring positive results.

The result of our desires should always point back to our glorious and loving Jesus.

> This is the confidence we have in approaching God: that if we ask anything according to his will, he hears us. And if we know that he hears us—whatever we ask—we know that we have what we asked of him.
>
> —1 John 5:14–15

> Delight yourself in the Lord and he will give you the desires of your heart.
>
> —Psalm 37:4

A Place and Time

Every day I look forward to spending time with the Holy Spirit. I noticed that my desire to be with Him was being frustrated with my inability to focus and give Him my undivided attention. In the beginning, I found it difficult to find time to spend with the Holy Spirit. I tried evenings, afternoons, mornings, but nothing seemed to work. Another problem I encountered was my inability to focus on Him. I spent too much time fighting my own thoughts and trying to remove all types of distractions. These struggles led to frustration.

I noticed that the desire I had to be with Him was being slowly devoured by my daily struggles. One morning as I struggled to concentrate on the Holy Spirit, He brought to my attention a new concept. He wanted me to meet Him at a specific place and time. Since I complied with His direction, my time with the Holy Spirit has not been the same. With less difficulty, I can step into the presence of the Lord. The Holy Spirit continued to share with me how the Old and New Testaments are full of accounts of people whose lives reinforce this concept of meeting God at a certain time and place.

For example, in the Book of Genesis we read about Abraham: "Early the next morning Abraham got up and returned to the place where he had stood before the Lord" (Gen. 19:27). In the Book of Exodus we read about another person who had an intimate relationship with God: "Now Moses used to take a tent and pitch it outside the camp some distance away, calling it the 'tent of meeting.' Anyone inquiring of the LORD would go to the tent of meeting outside the camp" (Exod. 33:7). In the Book of Mark we read about Jesus and his relationship with the Father: "Very early in the morning, while it was still dark, Jesus got up, left the house and went off to a solitary place, where He prayed" (Mark 1:35).

By adopting this concept, in my pursuit of intimacy with the Holy Spirit, of seeking God at a particular time and in a certain place I slowly began to notice a positive change in my spiritual growth. I did not see the change immediately. In the beginning of the journey, my mind and body fought against my spirit's pursuit of God.

The most common problems I faced were the wandering of my mind and experiencing physical discomfort based upon hunger, thirst, or unacceptable change in the room temperature. These distractions created a very uncomfortable struggle between my mind, body, and spirit.

After several visits to the same place around the same time, I finally surrendered to the Holy Spirit's direction to meet Him there. And I began to experience a wonderful communion without interruption with the Holy Spirit. During those intimate moments, I really touched His heart and He touched mine.

Personal reflections

Setting a place and time to meet with God helped me become more consistent in my walk with the Lord. It helped me to pursue my daily reading of the Bible and prayer. As creatures of habit, it is good to be intentional in separating a specific time to be with the Lord daily.

A place and time sets up the stage to remove all distractions, training our mind and body to completely submit to the Holy Spirit.

God Is a Multi-Dimensional God

The more time I spend with the Holy Spirit the more I became aware of all my weaknesses. I realized that my days were full of battles between my body, mind, and spirit. I felt the desires of my flesh were equally as strong as my desires to please the Lord. My constant battles were with simple things such as controlling my eyes from looking at things that did not bring me closer to God, or my mind from wandering and daydreaming of things that were not of God.

One morning as I spent time with the Holy Spirit He shared with me the idea of God being multi-dimensional. He reminded me that all creation is seen through a 3-D lens and that my ability to be effective in the body of Christ depends upon maintaining a multi-dimensional pursuit of the Father. He used the following points as examples.

Point one—the Trinity

The Book of Ephesians (Part I) describes the three Persons of the Trinity:

- God the Father who is credited with the work of creation. (See Genesis 1:1; 14:22.)

- God the Son who is the principal agent in applying the work of redemption to humanity. (See Ephesians 2.)

- God the Holy Spirit who is the deposit or first installment that guarantees our future inheritance. (See Ephesians 1:1–14.)

Point two—the temple

In the Book of Exodus (chapter 25) and in First Kings (chapter 6), we find a description of the pattern for the temple of Moses. God gave the builder a very detailed blueprint for building the temple. The plan called for three main areas:

- The Outer Court
- The Holy Place
- The Most Holy Place

Point three—human beings

In the Book of Genesis (Part I) and in First Thessalonians 5:23, we find a description of the three parts that comprise a human being:

- Body
- Soul
- Spirit

I was amazed with the revelation that our God was a "3-D God." As the Holy Spirit reminded me once again, He expects us to pursue Him in a multi-dimensional approach.

Point four—Christian disciplines

The three areas of Christian discipline are designed to work best as they are combined. An inability to maintain a balance of these three elements can create within us a weak foundation that can stop us from becoming an effective Christian. These disciplines include:

- The Bible
- Prayer
- Fasting

As the Holy Spirit continued to share, I discovered that each of these areas has a different purpose and is uniquely designed to strengthen us as believers. This can only be achieved when:

- The Bible becomes our living source of examples and confirmation of God's abilities.

- We understand that prayer is our only channel of communication with God (the Father, Son, and Holy Spirit).

- Fasting is given its rightful place in our lives. The purpose is to attract the attention of God. As a spiritual discipline, fasting can help us focus more intensely on God, increasing our ability to concentrate mentally. As a result, we become more sensitive to the things of the Holy Spirit.

The more the Holy Spirit shared with me about God's being a balanced God the more I realized that my daily battles were the result of an unbalanced pursuit of God. The more I tuned into prayer, reading the Bible, and fasting, the more fruitful my days were. The energy and time I spent fighting the desires of my flesh focused on maintaining a balanced approach to God.

A balanced approach to God will cause us to be fruitful and effective in our daily walk with Him.

Our potential in having a relationship with God is based on how strong our foundation is, which only comes from maintaining a balanced approach to God

Personal reflections

I learned that God wants us to have a solid foundation. It is not about how fast I can go or how much I am doing for the Lord, even though He wants us to be fruitful followers. His main concern is that we approach Him in a balanced manner. I cannot be effective as a Christian if I am lacking in reading the Bible, praying, and fasting. As my senior pastor, Scott Hagan, once said, "I want to finish well."

THREE TYPES OF FRIENDSHIPS

During my walk with the Holy Spirit I have surrounded myself with many good friends. Without realizing what I was doing, I made sure that my friends were just like me. This selection of friends encouraged me to become critical of those different from me. I never noticed my behavior and how it was destroying other peoples' lives by excluding them and categorizing them as living on "a lower level" than my friends and I were living. One morning, the Holy Spirit shared with me the concept of *three types of friendships.*

In the Book of Proverbs we read: "He who walks with the wise grows wise, but a companion of fools suffers harm " (Prov. 13:20). I realized that although my friends were good Christians, they were a very exclusive group; developing within me an unrealistic expectation of others. The Holy Spirit helped me to understand that the quality of my growth did not depend on the quantity but on the variety of my friendships. My goal should be to surround myself with people who give my life balance and provide *the three types of friendships* that should be found in the lives of every believer. These types of friendships include the *hungry,* the *equally-minded,* and the *giver.*

The "Hungry"

The "hungry" person is someone who is usually in a crisis or in need of help emotionally, physically, or spiritually. I was hesitant to associate with people who were different from me, but I did not allow my fears and concerns to keep me from getting to know the Holy Spirit better.

The Holy Spirit continued to explain the benefits of "the hungry friendship." This type of friendship provides a place where one can exercise God's love while at the same time remaining humble. However, He warned me that by surrounding myself with too many "hungry friendships" I could create imbalance in my life and thus place my walk with the Lord in jeopardy. I should not try to meet every hungry person's needs or otherwise I could become empty and spiritually drained.

The "Equally-Minded"

The equally-minded person is someone who is on the same level spiritually as you are. Unconsciously, I have made an effort for most of my Christian walk to surround myself with this type of friendship. I spent most of my days cultivating "equally-minded friendships." As a result, I noticed our behavior resembled the conduct of a family of monkeys. While watching the Discovery Channel, I noticed that apes spend most of their days removing bugs from each others' bodies. This behavior creates an environment that is safe, without presenting any real opportunities for growth to take place. The Holy Spirit revealed to me that such friendship environments will give impetus to the spirit of pride.

The "Giver"

The "giver" friendship is a mentor who has developed an intimate relationship with the Holy Spirit. It is very important to include some "giver" friends within your circle of friendships. But be mindful not to surround yourself with too many people of this group to the point that all you do is receive knowledge and wisdom from them.

The risk involved with exclusively surrounding yourself with "giver" friends, the Holy Spirit continued to explain, is that these relationships will cause you to eventually resemble a leech attached to a person. I learned while swimming in small pools of water as a child that the characteristic of a leech is to suck as much blood out of its victim as possible. A leech will not stop sucking blood until the object to which it is attached is completely empty. A believer's life will become unbalanced when he surrounds himself with too many "giver" friendships from which he or she "sucks" life, causing them to become spiritually lazy and "overweight."

The Holy Spirit continued to reveal that a proper relationship balance could be attained by having some friends that are hungry, some that are equally-minded, and some that are givers. I have learned that all of us have a purpose in the kingdom of God and that no one is more important than another. The Holy Spirit also reminded me that each of these types of friendships alone can become an obstacle to my pursuit of intimacy, but when properly balanced, they can become a bridge to a deeper level of intimacy with the Holy Spirit.

The "hungry friendship" will provide a wonderful opportunity for God's love to be demonstrated through me, requiring me to humble myself as well. The "equally-minded friendship" will provide a safe place to express frustration and concerns, a safe haven to express myself without fear of being misunderstood. The "giver friendship" will make sure that my spiritual strength is enhanced while developing a closer relationship with Jesus Christ.

Our God is a multi-dimensional God, and He expects us to experience spiritual growth in different levels of intimacy.

Personal reflections

I learned that God wants us to reflect His heart in all areas of life, including our friendships. It is easy to stay away from those who look, think, and behave in a different manner from us, but God wants us to be inclusive of all people. It is a good reminder to maintain a symmetric approach to our selection of friends. I am convinced that to be 100 percent effective as a Christian, father, husband and friend, we must be inclusive of all people, regardless of their gender, race or spiritual level.

LEVELS WITHIN HIS INTIMACY

During my first year of pursuing the Holy Spirit, He would talk to me and I would feel His presence during prayer. However, at one point a month went by when, during prayer, I did not hear His voice or feel His presence. I began to think that perhaps I had said something and offended the Holy Spirit.

But I never lost the devotional time with Him. As the days and then weeks went by without hearing His voice or feeling his presence, I began to feel more and more lonely. Questions would arise in my mind concerning why our relationship had changed.

Then one day, during my prayer time, the Holy Spirit spoke His first words after His long period of silence. I was like a kid in a room full of candy, unable to contain my excitement. The first thing I said was, "You're back!" As we talked He let me know that He was always by my side, but that He had needed to be silent for a time. I asked Him, "Why?" He responded, "I don't take my intimacy or my relationship with any person lightly. My detachment from you was to allow you to prove that you really wanted to be intimate with Me, that you valued our relationship."

While reading the Book of Deuteronomy, the Holy Spirit shared with me how God administered the same test to another group of people:

> Remember how the LORD your God led you all the way in the desert these forty years, to humble you and to test you in order to know what was in your heart, whether or not you would keep His commands.
> —DEUTERONOMY 8:2

I was relieved to know that I did not do anything wrong. He continued to explain: "As you get closer to me there will be times when I am going to be detached from you. The purpose of My detachment is to protect the intimacy of our relationship."

At that moment He reminded me again of the verse: "And do not grieve the Holy Spirit of God, with whom you were sealed for the day of redemption" (Eph. 4:30).

He continued to share with me, "The closer you get to Me the greater the chances that you have to harm Me. I am a real Person. I have feelings and emotions. I can get hurt. In order to protect you from damaging our relationship, I have divided the intimacy I offer at different levels. Every time you reach another level of intimacy with Me I will remove myself so you can search Me. You can prove that you are not content with the level of intimacy that you have with Me."

He reminded me that these levels did not represent the importance of one person over another. It represented an escalating level of intimacy that He offers everyone.

In the beginning when the Holy Spirit shared this concept with me I was surprised. How can it be? How can the Creator of the universe come to our level? From my walk with the Lord I realized that this is the beauty of our God; even though He didn't need to become vulnerable, He did in order to penetrate our close-minded view of Him, of a God who is unreachable and untouchable, without feelings and emotions. Ephesians 4:30 reminds us that we must be sensitive to Him as in any other relationship that we value.

Personal reflections

I learned that intimacy is not a destination, it is a process. We must continually pursue a deeper level of intimacy with Jesus. God does not want us to ever think we "have arrived." Apostle Paul said it best in the Book of Philippians:

> I press on toward the goal to win the prize for which God has called me heavenward in Christ Jesus.
> —PHILIPPIANS 3:14

MUCH MORE THAN ELEMENTARY

In the Book of Corinthians, the apostle Paul talks about the different levels of maturity with God when he states, "I gave you milk, not solid food, for you were not yet ready for it. Indeed, you are still not ready" (1 Cor. 3:2). And in the Book of Hebrews we read: "Therefore let us leave the elementary teachings about Christ and go on to maturity, not laying again the foundation of repentance from acts that lead to death, and of faith in God, instruction about baptisms, the laying on of hands, the resurrection of the dead, and eternal judgment" (Heb. 6:1–3).

I remember attending elementary school, which was followed by middle school, high school, and college. Each level of education exposed me to new concepts and ideas to challenge my understanding in various areas, such as algebra. During my first years of college, I realized that all the concepts and ideas learned in the lower levels of my education were just the beginning and could not compare to what I would learn in college. But I also realized that without the basics concepts learned early in my education, I would not have been prepared for the challenges of college.

As we mentioned, the Book of Hebrews describes what God considers to be elementary teachings:

- Repentance
- Faith in God
- Baptism
- Laying on of hands
- The resurrection of the dead
- Eternal judgment

I recognized that, though I had advanced through the college level academically, I was stuck at the elementary level, spiritually. God had much more to offer and I wanted to find out what it was. The Holy Spirit has revealed to me that only through Him can we be taught the "advanced courses" of God. This process of learning begins through intimacy we experience with Him.

I was reminded that regardless of the level of intimacy, no believer is more holy than another person. We must remember that God looks at you and me as a finished product through the lenses of Ephesians 2:6, and God raised us up with Christ and seated us with Him in the heavenly realms in Christ Jesus.

However, we must continue in our pursuit to be like Jesus and make ourselves ready for our Bridegroom.

> Let us rejoice and be glad and give him glory for the wedding of the Lamb has come, and his bride has made herself ready.
>
> —REVELATION 19:7

Personal reflections

I was astounded to realize that my whole Christian life I have focused only on elementary teachings. I learned that even though elementary teachings are important as they serve as the foundation for my life in God, there is much more that God wants us to discover. It would be a waste for us to live and die without ever experiencing the fullness of God.

ONE LEVEL AT A TIME

Each level of intimacy has different requirements and the potential to positively or negatively affect the kingdom of God.

The following example provides a description of a person who is at phase one.

- A person who is at this phase of developing an intimate relationship with the Holy Spirit normally has not completely surrendered his will to the leadership of Jesus Christ. A person can resist the guidance of the Holy Spirit at any level because we have been given free will to either resist or obey God.

God's Word says "If we claim to be without sin, we deceive ourselves and the truth is not in us" (1 John 1:8). As we walk through the different levels of intimacy with Jesus, we should expect the level of trust to increase as the relationship deepens. The following points remind us what to expect in the beginning of the relationship:

- A limited level of responsibility and trust from the Holy Spirit. This will grow as the believer draws closer to Him.

- Some areas of a believer's life will not be surrendered to the leadership of the Holy Spirit. He would not allow this lack of surrender in other Christians that are at a deeper level of intimacy with Jesus.

Personal reflections

I used to love watching movies that were filled with violence and profanity. One morning during my time with the Lord, the Holy Spirit asked me to give up R-rated movies. I did not think much of it and agreed to do so without processing the question. Later during the week, I decided to watch a movie when the Holy Spirit questioned me, "Do you know the rating of that movie?"

I replied, "No, but it is one of the movies I normally watch and I am sure is not R-rated."

"Take the tape out and look," He replied.

To my surprise the movie was rated R. The immediate thought that crossed my mind was to ask Him how He knew what the movie was rated. Of course, I responded by answering my own question: "He is God."

During the next few days I discarded all the R-rated movies I owned. There were only a few movies left after I completed this task—I was not a happy person.

The next morning the Holy Spirit explained why He made this request of me. He said, "I will remove anything that competes with me." It is not the rating of the movies, but the fact that you identify with many of the characters in R-rated movies more than you identify with me."

Before we move to a higher level of intimacy we may be required to release and submit new areas of our life to Him. As we move into deeper relationship with Him, anything that competes with the things of God must eventually be discarded.

Why are we required to surrender new areas to God? As a believer moves closer to God, he will be held more accountable for his actions that can negatively impact God's will. We must remove anything that competes with His affection. Before we move to a deeper, more intimate relationship with Jesus, He will ask us to release those areas we have not surrendered to God. There is a risk involved in not submitting every area of our lives to God as He reveals them to us. We always have the freedom to obey or resist Him, affecting the quality of our relationship with Him.

Obedience and trust should come naturally as we progress into a deeper relationship with God. Our ability to develop and maintain an intimate relationship with Jesus is very much dependant on our willingness to obey Him. The following two points remind us how obedience affects our relationship with God.

- When we surrender to God, we submit specific areas of our life to the Father and step into a greater level of intimacy with Him.

- *When we are disobedient,* our spiritual growth diminishes and we are unable to experience a greater level of intimacy with the Father.

We can expect negative results from not submitting areas requested by God. Our decision not to surrender and obey the leading of the Holy Spirit has permanent and long-lasting consequences to the continual growth of our relationship with Jesus. The following three areas are examples of the natural consequences from not surrendering our life to Jesus.

- When we refuse to release an area we choose not to move forward and grow spiritually.

- When we do not obtain a greater level of intimacy our Christian journey can become routine and boring.

- We will never experience a higher level of responsibility or intimacy when we resist God.

God will continue to use us (even though we refuse to move forward) within the limitations that come with that level of relationship. Also, the act of hiding from God results in a gap in the relationship, also known as *sin*. The Holy Spirit reminded me that this process of increasing to a higher level of intimacy continues as long as we are on this planet. He continued to share what our goals should be:

As we continue to move into a deeper relationship with the Lord we should continue to press forward, not relying on past experiences, but renewing our desire and love for Jesus daily. The apostle Paul declared this passion to know God: "Not that I have already obtained all this, or have already been made perfect, but I press on to take hold of that for which Christ Jesus took hold of me. Brothers, I do not consider myself yet to have taken hold of it. But one thing I do: Forgetting what is behind and straining toward what is ahead, I press on toward the goal to win the prize for which God has called me heavenward in Christ Jesus" (Phil. 3:12–14).

We should exercise ourselves in the following two areas:

- To press forward
- To help those on different levels

Do not judge others. God knows the heart of every person and He understands what is required from every person at each level.

Personal reflections

I was reminded once again that our relationship with the Lord is no different than our relationship with other people. We must continue to grow and release areas that could hinder our relationship with God. Our inability to change and grow can create a gap in our relationship with God, friends, and family.

Salvation vs. Relationship

The development of my relationship with the Holy Spirit is similar in many ways to my relationship with my spouse. For example, I must continually work on improving the communication and making sure that we spend quality time together.

For many years, I confused the definitions of salvation and relationship. My approach to developing a relationship with the Lord was similar in my approach to receiving salvation. I thought all I needed to do was ask for intimacy, like I had asked to receive the miracle of salvation, and somehow my relationship with God would come into a place of intimacy. After several failed attempts to develop a relationship with the Holy Spirit by using the "salvation approach," I gave up trying.

Since then, I have come to understand that salvation is a gift, but relationship always costs you something. God has promised us eternal life in Christ through the gift of salvation. But He never promised us a free ride to intimacy. By understanding my relationship with the Holy Spirit through my relationship with my wife, I have been able to discern that intimacy and growth depend on how much we are willing to invest in our relationship.

No relationship can survive without constant communication and hard work devoted to developing the relationship.

Personal reflections

Learning the difference between receiving the gift of salvation and developing intimate relationship with God has allowed me to be more effective in my approach to developing my relationship with God. Prior to understanding these differences, I spent most of my days frustrated with God for not giving me a free ride to an intimate relationship with Him. As my level of intimacy with Jesus grows, I must constantly remind myself that intimacy will cost me.

THE LOSS OF SENSITIVITY

Sensitivity is an ongoing topic of discussion in our home. My wife believes I am getting better at recognizing when I am being insensitive. Many times she thought that my approach to other people was too "business-like." Thanks to her support and continuous reminders, I am improving in learning to recognize when I am being insensitive to others.

The Holy Spirit has revealed more to me about the need for sensitivity. The apostle Paul declared of the Gentiles of his day: "Having lost all sensitivity, they have given themselves over to sensuality so as to indulge in every kind of impurity, with a continual lust for more" (Eph. 4:19).

The Holy Spirit has shown me that in order to maintain our sensitivity to Him we must continually spend quality time with Him. If we are unaware of our lack of sensitivity, we will not be protected from the consequences listed in the above scripture.

One of the many benefits of becoming more sensitive to the Holy Spirit is continual protection in all areas of our lives. God promises us protection from the following:

- A darkened perception of God's ways. For example, a distortion of the Word of God, interpreting it for the sake of one's own satisfaction.

- Hardening of our hearts.

Sensitivity to the Holy Spirit creates a mantle to make us resemble God's true righteousness and holiness. Always remember, sensitivity is not a place or destination, it is a process.

Personal reflections

Learning that I am accountable to increase my ability to be sensitive to the Holy Spirit and others around me has helped me grow in the Lord. Our inability to be sensitive to the Holy Spirit could remove God's mantle of protection in our lives.

STUDY GUIDE

SCRIPTURES FOR MEDITATION
Hebrews 5:11–14; 6:1–3
Hebrews 11:6
Mark 1: 35
Ephesians 1; 6:18
2 Timothy 3:15
Ephesians 4:17–19

SUMMARY STATEMENTS

- Expectations that come as a result of our relationship with the Holy Spirit will always have positive outcomes in our walk with the Lord.

- Establishing a specific place and time will teach our flesh to be silent during our time with the Lord.

- Our inability to move toward God in a multi-dimensional way will cause us to become less effective as Christians.

- Our foundation must include the reading of the Bible, prayer, and fasting.

- God can use our friendships to make us more effective in our walk with the Lord.

- If our friendships are unbalanced they can become an obstacle in our walk with the Lord.

- God created us for intimacy and friendship.

- Lack of sensitivity to the Holy Spirit is one of the reasons we do not experience God's presence in our lives.

- God's mantle of protection guarantees His investment in our lives.

QUESTIONS TO CONSIDER

1. Do you believe that scheduling a place and time to meet with the Lord would help you in developing an intimate relationship with Him? When would you be willing to meet with Him? If you already do so, how often do you meet with Him?

2. Which of the following best describes your time with the Lord? Explain.
   - Intimacy
   - Loneliness
   - Frustration
   - Other

3. Is God using you to your full potential?

4. How diverse is your list of friendships?

5. Do you believe that God wants us to diversify our friendships? Explain.

6. How do you think God would describe your level of obedience? Explain.

7. Describe the approach you are using to develop intimacy with Jesus. How effective is your approach?

8. How sensitive are you to the Holy Spirit?

Chapter 5

In His Presence

Enjoying Intimacy With God

THE VISIONS I am sharing with you give just a glimpse into the spiritual realm all around us. Heaven and hell are real, and the experiences I describe are told to remind you and me that our life on this earth is short and we have a responsibility to live a life pleasing to God.

Dancing in His Presence

The relationship that I have developed with the Holy Spirit has been requiring us to spend more time together. We began by spending one hour together every morning and still my spirit was not satisfied. One day, during my time with the Holy Spirit, He asked me to set apart a day to spend time with Him.

My reaction was, "A whole day?"

But I agreed to do it.

He also said, "I have one requirement. On this day you are

to use the time to fellowship with Me. Make no requests for yourself or others and do not eat anything." I knew the only day I had free to spend with him was Saturday. So I talked to my wife about it, knowing it would mean sacrificing our time together, and as always, she understood.

The day arrived for the Holy Spirit and me to spend our first Saturday together. I did not know what to expect. I brought with me as many books as I could find and my Bible to keep me occupied. During the afternoon I was singing some praise and worship songs. He asked me to dance in front of God the Father. This was the second time He had ever asked me to dance for Him. Still, I felt kind of silly dancing in that setting.

However, as I started to dance, I felt like I was being lifted up out of the room. I found myself standing on a cloud. The cloud was only big enough for me to stand alone. I continued dancing, but could not help but look at the cloud on which I was standing. I looked behind me and to my left and saw thousands of people standing, kneeling, dancing, and lying down on other clouds. For a second, I could not understand what this scene meant.

But the Lord answered my thoughts before I was able to articulate the question. He said, "These are my people when they come close to me." I understood that every time we set apart a time for the Lord, we are lifted up on a cloud and drawn closer into the presence of God. Soon my attention turned to a bright light that was coming from a distance and was illuminating everything that could be seen. It was a very bright light that was right in my face. I literally felt like I was standing in the presence of God.

The Lord said, "Look to your left." As I looked, there was an empty cloud. He said to me, "This cloud belongs to your wife." I understood that He was asking that this day be set aside to spend it with Him as a couple. And then all of a sudden I was back in my room. Those days we waited on God as a couple not only brought us closer to God, but also to each other.

Our obedience to the Lord always results in a better understanding of who He is.

Personal reflections

After this experience, all I wanted was to go back into the presence of the Lord. We all want to be in His presence; that is why we were created. Understanding that we have free access to walk into the presence of the Lord has given me the confidence I need to approach Him daily. I hope and pray that every person reading this book will experience the wonderful satisfaction found only in His Presence.

MY FIRST LOVE

On another occasion, as I waited before the Lord, I was supernaturally transported by two angels into the presence of God. I found myself in the midst of millions of heavenly beings. The overwhelming beauty of the surroundings was breathtaking. The angels were beautiful, like pressured diamonds. Their clothing was as white as the snow and brighter than the sun. The floor seemed to be a large crystal reflecting the bright light found in this place. I was amazed at the indescribable beauty all around me.

I had been in God's presence before, but there was something different about this place. I noticed that all the heavenly beings repeated a beautiful melody in one accord. They were praising the name of the Lord, saying, "Here comes our King of Kings!" In their faces you could see the anticipation and excitement as they continued to repeat, "Here comes our King of Kings."

Among the angelic beings was an angel who was assigned to announce the name of Jesus. More than a job, I understood it was an honor. It was his reward. His face became radiant and full of joy as he repeated the name of Jesus. It seemed like all heaven stopped every time the angel repeated the name of

Jesus. Shortly after the angel proclaimed the name of Jesus for a third time, every angel felt prostrate to the floor.

As I glanced around me, looking for an answer as to what had just happened, I noticed that the only person standing among millions of heavenly beings was me. The Holy Spirit walked next to me and whispered in my ear, "Jesus is about to enter the room." Then, there He was—Jesus. I could not take my eyes off Him. His presence overcame all the beauty of the surroundings. I noticed something different this time; He walked and interacted with the heavenly beings as a Man in authority. He wore a crown and a robe that represented glory, honor, authority, and power. He walked through the crowd toward where I was standing. As He came closer to me, my knees gave out and I felt prostrate.

Jesus tapped me on the shoulder and asked me to get up. He said to me, "You do not have to bow down in my presence. I call you friend." I stood up. He asked me to touch his hand and to stick my hands into His side. As I placed my hands into His side, it felt like I stuck my hands into a furnace. Jesus looked into my eyes and asked me, "Do you love me?" I was shocked that He asked me that question. Without hesitation, I replied, "Yes, Jesus you know that I love you." "Then feed my sheep," Jesus replied.

He asked me again, "Do you love me?" I looked at Him with a concerned look. "Lord, you know me better than anyone else, and you know that I love you." "Then feed my sheep," Jesus replied. He asked me the same question a third time, and I broke down weeping. He looked me in the eyes and allowed me to feel the love He has for all people, as He repeated the words, "Feed my sheep." In the Book of John 21:15–19 we find a similar story involving one of Jesus' disciples named Peter.

A year later, the Lord brought this vision to my mind as He explained what he meant by the question, "Do you love me?" In essence, He is asking you and me: "Do you cry when I cry? Do the things that make Me happy, make you happy? Are you passionate about the things that matter to Me?" I realized that my love for Jesus must go beyond initial affection. The Scriptures teach us to reflect the love of God in the earth:

> Jesus replied, "If anyone loves me, he will obey my teaching. My father will love him, and we will come to him and make our home with him.
>
> —JOHN 14:23

> This is how God showed his love among us: He sent his one and only Son into the world that we might live through him. This is love: not that we loved God, but that he loved us and sent his Son as an atoning sacrifice for our sins.
>
> —1 JOHN 4:9

Personal reflections

I spent many days, weeks, and months thinking about this vision. His question, "Do you love me?" continues to echo in my spirit to this day. For many years I saw myself as a person who loved the Lord with all his heart. After experiencing this vision, I realized that my love for the Lord had limitations. Can I say that I cry when Jesus cries, or do I get happy or angry for the things of which Jesus is passionate? We must continually reevaluate ourselves and answer those questions, because one day when we stand in His presence we are going to give an account of our love for Him.

IN THE LAST DAYS

One day during my prayer time I fell asleep. I found myself in a really dark place. I was following a group of eight or ten people. I knew it was very late, around 11:00 p.m. They were not aware of my presence. I noticed by the look on their faces there was a sense of urgency. Somehow I knew they needed to find something. I followed them throughout the night as they went from one place to another through a dark city.

I noticed that the condition of the city was in complete dis-
array. The houses were destroyed to the ground. There was no
sense of order; there was only chaos. It was the kind of chaos
that you can sometimes feel in your bones. I saw fear in the
peoples' eyes. They looked like they had lived in the woods for
years and years. Their clothes were really rough looking. They
seemed to have no concern for their physical appearance.

It was apparent that they had combined their forces to
search for something; it was also clear that there was a sense of
distrust among them. I followed them the whole night, trying
to make sense of what it was they were looking for. At times
they would dig into the ground and then they would remove
the rubble from the houses that were destroyed. As the night
came to an end they became more and more agitated.

Towards morning, but before daylight, the people went
down into the sewer system. The sewer system was destroyed;
it looked like a bomb had exploded, making the sewer more
like a hole in the ground. It was only big enough for them to
crawl from one place to the next. It did not look like an up-
to-date sewer system with open passageways. They spent the
day hiding in the sewer system. They talked among themselves and I understood from their conversation that there
was a time limit on what it was they needed to find—"the
clock was ticking!"

I noticed that we were not the only group in the same pre-
dicament; another group of people not too far away from us
was also hiding in the sewer. As I observed the other group
talking among themselves, they seemed to be joyful. I did not
observe this aspect in the other groups I had been watching to
see what was bringing them so much joy.

They were standing in a circle passing a piece of paper
among each other. As they passed the piece of paper, the
whole group would look at the person holding the paper with
mistrust. The paper was about 2 inches square and they were
being very careful with it. It looked as if the paper had been

recovered from a fire; the edges were burned.

I got close enough to see what was so important about this paper. I realized that this group had found what the group I had been following had been trying to find.

Then I recognized the paper they were holding. It was part of a page taken from the Bible. I could not tell what passage of scripture the paper contained because of the condition of the paper. But I saw them holding it as the most prized possession and kissing it like it was the most valuable possession that one could ever have. I could not comprehend their excitement because I was thinking to myself, "I have several Bibles at home, and in my church we have several hundred Bibles."

From my peripheral vision, I saw that the group I had been following was moving forward. I followed them again for several days. They seemed to follow the same routine, hiding in the daytime and searching during the night.

Somehow, one member of the group found a connection to someone outside the groups living in this underground world. He convinced the group to come with him and said that it was safe; they would be able to eat. I followed them and they walked into this really beautiful home. I remember seeing beautiful and expensive chandeliers hanging from the ceiling.

It really had an effect on me because I contrasted it with the grungy place where these people had been hiding. What a drastic change in their environment. It was not just a contrast in the environment, but in the people's appearance there. The people in the home were dressed in tuxedos. They were really friendly to the group that had been hiding, which I will refer to as "survivors."

The survivors sat down at a banquet table of food and they could walk up and down a buffet and take whatever they wanted to eat. Shortly after they had finished eating and drinking, soldiers came into the room and stood near the entrance. The survivors jumped up from the table and the soldiers shot many of them, killing them instantly. Only two managed to escape, but they were wounded. At this point, I immediately woke up from my dream. The Holy Spirit said to me, "Preserve Bibles."

Several weeks following this vision the Holy Spirit impressed on me the following scripture:

> "The days are coming", declares the Sovereign Lord, "when I will send a famine through the land—not a famine of food or a thirst for water, but a famine of hearing the words of the Lord. Men will stagger from sea to sea and wander from north to east, searching for the word of the Lord, but they will not find it."
>
> —Amos 8:11–12

Personal reflections

I must be diligent not only to read my Bible, but also to share it with those around me. Sometimes I forget that the Bible is living water and that there are many people around me who are thirsty. We must not become so comfortable with the content of the Bible that we forget how valuable it is to those who are thirsty and hungry for God.

> For the word of God is living and active. Sharper than any double-edged sword, it penetrates even to dividing soul and spirit, joints and marrow; it judges the thoughts and attitudes of the heart.
>
> —Hebrews 4:12

Hearing the word of God is a privilege.

A Horrible Place

Again, during my prayer time I fell into a deep sleep. I found myself in a place where there was no sense of time or order. The air was full of smoke. I could sense that it was not just smoke, it was a Presence! There were thousands, maybe millions of people. It was beyond a number that I could ever count. The people were not able to see me; however, they were able to see the person who was escorting me through the place.

I never saw the person who was next to me and I really didn't care, because I felt safe, secure, and loved. For some reason I knew that my guide was Jesus. Our feet never touched the ground; we were floating and walking on air. He took me through different rooms.

The people who were in this place seemed to be in agony and pain. They were naked, but most of their flesh was gone. It looked like chunks of flesh had been ripped from their bodies, even their faces. They had no sense of direction. They would walk around trying to find something. The pain I was able to see in the expressions on their faces was beyond the worst physical pain that could ever be experienced. It was like they understood why they were in this place and that there was no possible way for them to escape.

There was no joy, peace, or happiness in these people. However, in their pain, they seemed to find pleasure by inflicting pain upon others. There was no sense of friendship, but they would form attachments in order to cause even more pain to someone else. They jumped from one person to the next, biting, gouging, kicking, and mocking them.

Even while attacking their victim, they would often stop inflicting pain on the victim that had been singled out by the group and would start attacking each other within the group. On their faces you could see that for a second they would derive enjoyment from this horrible experience. This violent behavior was happening all over the place.

When I could not stand to watch them any longer, Jesus led me in another direction. As we were walking together, one of them approached Jesus. He reached out his hands as in an act of begging for mercy. It was as if this person was saying to Jesus, "Please, help me, get me out of here!"

My heart was broken at that point. I knew in my spirit that there was no way for them to be released from their torment even though I wished there was a way for them to escape from their hell. Jesus proceeded to show me the rest of the place. My heart was so moved; I never imagined that people could inflict so much pain upon one another.

We came to a place where a man was standing behind a table. Previously, no one there had been able to see me. But for some reason, this man was able to see me. He looked at me with a sense of pride in his eyes. I understood he was the leader.

Some of the people were brought to the leader. They were placed on the table and the leader would inflict them with pain beyond comprehension. They would grab the persons' hands and pluck out their fingernails one by one. As the person was screaming, whoever was standing around the table would start laughing. The leader looked at me and snickered saying, "I am in control!"

Then Jesus took me to another area. It seemed to be the entrance. The people that were walking into this area looked pretty clean and had on all of their clothes. Their flesh was completely intact. But there was a group of people that were already waiting for them, similar to a pack of wolves waiting to devour a lamb. They would jump on top of them and literally devour them.

At that point, my heart was so broken, I could not take it anymore. I thought to myself, there cannot be anything worse than this place. Jesus answered my thoughts with a soft smile, like He was saying, "If you only if knew what else was in this place." My Jesus knew that my heart could not stand it anymore, and suddenly I was no longer there.

When I awakened, I heard a voice crying, "Compassion." The Bible is clear about the wonderful compassion of our God. Peter declares: "The Lord is not slow in keeping his promise, as some understand slowness. He is patient with you, not wanting anyone to perish, but everyone to come to repentance" (2 Peter 3:9).

However, Jesus gave us a glimpse of a place called hell in the following account:

> There was a rich man who was dressed in purple and fine linen and lived in luxury every day. At his gate was laid a beggar named Lazarus, covered with sores and longing to eat what fell from the rich man's table. Even the dogs came and licked his sores. The time came when the beggar died and the angels carried him to Abraham's side. The rich man also died and was buried. In hell, where he was in torment, he looked up and saw Abraham far away, with Lazarus by his side. So he called to him, "Father Abraham, have pity on me and send Lazarus to dip the tip of his finger in water and cool my tongue, because I am in agony in this fire." But Abraham replied, "Son, remember that in your lifetime you received your good things, while Lazarus received bad things, but now he is comforted here and you are in agony. And besides all this, between us and you a great chasm has been fixed, so that those who want to go from here to you cannot, nor can anyone cross over from there to us." He answered, "Then I beg you, Father, send Lazarus to my father's house, for I have brothers. Let him warn them, so that they will not also come to this place of torment." Abraham replied, "They have Moses and the Prophets, let them listen to them." "No, father Abraham," he said, "but if someone from the dead goes to them, they will repent." He said to him, "If they do not listen to Moses and the Prophets, they will not be convinced even if someone rises from the dead."
>
> —Luke 16:19–31

Personal reflections

I have never experienced the pain of being separated from my immediate family. The place I just described is full of people separated from their loved ones and, more importantly, separated from God. We were created to be with God. It is inconceivable how evil human beings can be when we are separated from God. Jesus died so you and I can once again be restored to having a relationship with Him. Do not miss this opportunity. Unlike the people in the accounts you have just read, we do not have to experience eternal separation from our Father. We were meant to be with our Creator for eternity. Our Father is an all-loving God who is not willing that any should perish, but He must leave the choice to be with Him "in paradise" to each one of us.

GOD'S TOOLS

One afternoon, I woke up around 6:00 p.m. from taking a nap. From the moment I opened my eyes, I felt deeply depressed, anxious, and worried. It was like an outside force was pressing hard against my chest. I grabbed my Bible and went to the extra bedroom in our house to spend time alone with the Lord.

It felt like I needed to push to get some words out of my mouth. The environment felt very heavy around me. As I lifted my voice to heaven, I saw a window open in front of me. I could see a vision of myself. I saw what looked like hundreds of arrows coming towards me. All over my body, I was being hit by arrow after arrow.

After looking carefully, I noticed that the arrows were actually short creatures. As the creatures made contact with my body they attached to my skin; immediately they grew tentacles that spread all over my body. Each creature had a title attached to them; I saw depression, anxiety, and confusion.

From behind me, I heard the voice of the Holy Spirit telling me to use the weapons I had. Instantly, a Bible appeared in my right hand. The Bible was no bigger than my hand. The Holy Spirit continued His instruction: "Use your faith." From the center of my chest, a beam of light came straight out and made contact with the Bible.

At that moment, the Bible became alive and it started growing. As the Bible grew, the creatures that were attached to my body fell off. Light radiated from the Bible forming a protective shield that covered my whole body. This shield was alive and reacted to the attack by bouncing the creatures off. The shield was transparent, allowing me to see how the creatures were supernaturally prevented from reaching me. The vision ended and I was back in my room praying.

I noticed that I was not feeling down or depressed anymore. The Holy Spirit reminded me to daily use my faith so that the enemy's attacks would not reach me.

Personal reflections

We cannot be an effective Christian without the protection that comes from reading and applying the truths of the Bible in our daily lives. Of course, the Scriptures teach us about putting on the whole armor of God to defeat the enemy. In Ephesians 6:16 we read: "In addition to all this, take up the shield of faith with which you can extinguish all the flaming arrows of the evil one."

It is essential that we understand who we are in Christ and what weapons we have at our disposal in order to be a successful Christian, parent, spouse, and friend.

God has given us all the necessary weapons to be successful.

Compassion

During my personal devotional time, I found myself floating inside a tunnel. Next to me was a person holding my hand. As before, I was so overwhelmed by what I was seeing that I did not concern myself with who was holding my hand.

We were about 400 feet above the ground. Below us were people lined up—there seemed to be millions of people assembled. As I scoped the area with my eyes to estimate the number of people, I realized they were beyond my ability to count. The people seemed to be in a deep sleep, as if they were zombies. They walked slowly at a synchronized pace.

I thought to myself, "Where are all these people heading?" The person holding my hand responded, "I will show you." It was as if the person holding my hand could not wait for me to ask.

Immediately, at a speed faster than light, we flew to the beginning of the line. The people were falling into a hole in the ground; I was not able to see the bottom of the hole. I noticed that they were not aware of where they were going until they started falling. As they fell, it seemed their eyes were opened and they understood what was happening. I wanted to stop them. I wanted to scream and warn them about what was in front of them, but the person holding my hand made me realize that there was nothing I could do at this point.

Tears started flowing from my eyes. While I was crying, the person next to me pointed down into the hole and everything zoomed into focus about five feet from me. I was able to see the bottom of the hole. Millions of people were in what looked like a lake of fire. The flames seemed to be alive, holding the people inside the hole.

They cried, cursed, and reached out trying to come out of that pit of hell—all to no avail. I wept like a baby as I looked at the faces of the people in the flames. Slowly the scene started to fade away, and we were once again above ground with the line of people. Then the person next to me whispered, "Compassion."

Right after that, we started to fly. We were moving at an incalculable speed. I found myself on top of a longer row of people. Here, there were at least one hundred thousand times more people than we had seen inside the tunnel. They had their hands up as if they were singing and praising. As I scanned the place with my eyes, I noticed that they were worshiping Someone who was sitting at a distance.

I was unable to clearly see whom they were worshiping, but a bright light came from where the Person was sitting. That light penetrated everything around it. Then, I noticed that we were moving again, and once more I found myself looking down into the hole. I must have gone back and forth three to four times to look down into that hole while the person holding my hand repeated, "Compassion."

By the third time, I cried out, "No more please!" Immediately, I was back in my bedroom. I cried for a long time. Even today the images of the people in that hole still have not faded from my memory.

Jesus is a compassionate God.

Personal reflections

> For it is light that makes everything visible. This is why it is said: "Wake up, o sleeper, rise from the dead, and Christ will shine on you." Be very careful, then how you live not as unwise but as wise.
>
> —EPHESIANS 5:14

The Bible says that Jesus while on the earth was moved with compassion for those who did not have a relationship with Him. I pray and hope that we will make the most of every opportunity, because there are many around us who are blind and in darkness. May the Lord help us to have compassion for those who do not know Him so they can be part of His family.

FAITH

Shortly after waking up I felt very anxious about the future. One morning I grabbed my Bible and went to spend time with the Lord.

Shortly after kneeling down, a window opened up in front of me and I found myself standing on a flat round surface with Jesus. In front of us were other surfaces similar to the one on which we were standing. I noticed that none of the surfaces were connected to each other. With nothing under them, the flat, round surfaces were suspended in the air and encompassed by darkness. The pieces of land were farther away from me and the distance between each of them was also greater.

Jesus looked at me and told me to follow Him. Immediately, He was standing across from me on another surface. Many questions crossed my mind as I walked toward the edge of where I was standing.

I looked down and became afraid because of the darkness all around the flat surfaces. I thought to myself, *How did Jesus walk to the other side if there is nothing connecting each point?* He looked at me while extending his hand and said, "COME!"

I stood there without moving as Jesus asked, "Are you going to stand there or are you going to come?"

I closed my eyes because I did not want to see what I was about to do. As I stepped forward, a bridge appeared under my feet connecting the two points. My confidence rose in a matter of seconds and I started to run toward Jesus. When I reached the other end, Jesus was standing there with a big smile on His face!

He told me, "Now you are to keep walking forward and I will always be waiting for you on the other side. Keep your eyes open for any cracks in the pathway." I remembered the scripture that says, "We walk by faith and not by sight" (2 Cor. 5:7).

Our Christian walk is similar to a road or a pathway. Jesus taught his disciples that He is the Way; the apostle John records that affirmation: "Jesus answered, 'I am the way and the truth and the life. No one comes to the Father except through me'" (John 14:6).

The psalmist referred to this path of life as well: "Your word is a lamp to my feet and a light for my path" (Ps. 119:105). In the Book of Proverbs we read, "The path of life leads upward for the wise to keep him from going down to the grave" (Prov.

15:24). And again, "The way of the sluggard is blocked with thorns, but the path of the upright is a highway" (Prov. 15:19). Isaiah declared, "The path of the righteous is level; O upright one, you make the way of the righteous smooth" (Isa. 26:7).

In this vision, the Holy Spirit gave me a visual illustration of this path. During my time with the Lord, I saw what seemed to be a road and on it were millions of people from all backgrounds and languages. Everyone was walking in the same direction. I was floating, as the Holy Spirit held my hand, on top of this highway that seemed to have no end.

As I looked down, the Holy Spirit said, "Every believer from around the world is on this road." I soon understood that it was the path of life, the walk of faith required of all Christians. I noticed that this road was divided into different sections. In the beginning of the road people were walking very slowly, while others were standing and looking around. Ahead I saw people helping each other; as one person would fall to the ground, someone would pick him up.

However, in other areas of the road there were a few people preventing others from walking forward by standing in their way and blocking their path. In some areas, the surface had cracks and holes. Many were stuck in the cracks and some other people were afraid to jump the holes. Some of the sections of the road were missing. The gap became an obstacle to many people, as they stood there confused, but others walked right through the gaps as if somehow there was an invisible bridge connecting the gaps.

I noticed that some people were walking fast, hopping, and running. Some looked very happy and others did not seem to be enjoying the process. God was very sad and allowed me to feel the sadness in His heart as we watched how some of the people on the road did all they could to stop others from moving forward, hindering them from pursuing God's destiny for their lives. He was also sad to see others not expressing any concern for the people around them. Along each section of the path, the people had different strengths and abilities. As I watched each person from above, I could not help but experience some mixed emotions. I asked God, "Am I one of them?"

The Holy Spirit answered, "Yes, every believer is there, including you." I understood more clearly the words of the apostle Paul: "I have fought the good fight, I have finished the race, I have kept the faith" (2 Tim. 4:7).

Personal reflections

Our society reinforces the concept of being self-sufficient. It contends that in that way we should be able to manage all the struggles we must face in our lifetime. In contrast, Jesus asked us to rely on His abilities to be successful in life. I must say that one of the most difficult areas of my relationship with God is to give Him control of my life and trust completely that He is going to take care of my family and me. The story I described above reminds us that our Christian walk should depend 100 percent in God's ability to protect us and to provide for us. We will definitely have many opportunities to learn to trust and have faith in God as we walk forward on that path of life. I hope and pray that we will make the most of every opportunity.

Our faith is a result of our relationship with God.

OUR WALK

On this day, shortly after entering the prayer room, I fell asleep. I found myself looking down at a valley. At the bottom of this valley, Jesus was seated with about a hundred people encircling him. The people seated in the circle were quite taken by the knowledge, beauty, quietness, strength, and wisdom radiating from Him. Jesus was giving Himself to them, strengthening them. His body radiated a beautiful light that illuminated as far as my eyes could see. What a picture! I just wanted to set my tent next to Jesus and live happily ever after.

I saw people coming down into the valley toward Jesus.

They looked like they had just come from a war. Their faces showed different expressions: sorrow, despair, anguish, concern, disappointment. But as they came closer to Jesus their expressions changed; they became alive, full of joy and peace.

I decided to go and see where these people were coming from. As I walked away from Jesus and those seated around him, I saw a war raging. The light radiating from Jesus covered a wide area in the shape of a circle and came to an end as it met darkness. There the battle ensued.

As I walked around the edge of the circle of light, I noticed thousands of people on the edge outside the circle, in the darkness, stretching out their arms. I was not able to see why they were stretching out their arms, so I walked closer to them. Outside, the perimeter of the circle there was complete darkness; I could hardly see. But there, beyond the light radiating from Jesus, were millions of people trying to get inside the circle. They could not because other forces stopped them from doing so. These people had no eyes and no sense of direction; it seemed as though just by instinct they wanted to come toward the light. For a few seconds, I saw the reflection of my face in those trying to break through the darkness into the light. From within the circle of light, thousands of people were doing all they could to pull those outside into the circle. What a battle!

Those inside the circle were getting weaker. In their faces I was able to see their fatigue and concern, hoping that reinforcement would come soon. I thought to myself, "I need to do something. How can I help?"

I ran down toward Jesus as I passed those who were just released from fighting. I wanted to remind those who were seated around Jesus not to forget what was going on around them. Some of them, as soon as they regained strength, went back to the battle. Others seemed to have forgotten that they too had once walked in darkness.

Later, as I meditated about this vision, the Holy Spirit spoke to me. He wanted me to remember where I came from and not to become so comfortable with the beauty of being close to Jesus that I forget about those who still need salvation.

Personal reflections

In our Christian walk, we hope to live a life pleasing to God. The best way to fulfill the Bible in our lives is to help others and to help spread the gospel to those who live in darkness. Let's not become so at ease within our comfort zone that we forget to share the good news of Jesus Christ. Consider the apostle Paul's reminder of where we came from:

> As for you, you were dead in your transgressions and sins, in which you used to live when you followed the ways of this world and of the ruler of the kingdom of the air, the spirit who is now at work in those who are disobedient. All of us also lived among them at one time, gratifying the cravings of our sinful nature and following its desires and thoughts. Like the rest, we were by nature objects of wrath. But because of his great love for us, God, who is rich in mercy, made us alive with Christ even when we were dead in transgressions—it is by grace you have been saved.
>
> —EPHESIANS 2: 1–5

Study Guide

Scriptures for Meditation
2 Samuel 6:14
Amos 8:11–12
Psalm 100
Psalm 119:105
Matthew 22:2–14
Luke 16:19–31
John 15:13–15
2 Corinthians 5:7
Ephesians 6:10–18
Philippians 2:10–11; 3:20
Hebrews 4:12–13
2 Peter 2:4–10; 3:9
Jude 1:24
Revelation 19:9; 20:10; 21:1–8; 22:12–17

Summary Statements

- It brings great joy to the Father every time we make time for Him.

- We must not let our Bibles sit on our bookshelves and collect dust.

- There is a place called hell, described in the Bible, where pain and suffering go beyond the physical realm.

- The Bible explains that complete separation from God is the worst pain any one of us can ever experience.

- God has made available different weapons we can use to be successful as a Christian; they can be found as we read the Bible.

- We have been given the choice to decide where we want to spent eternity.

- God is a good Father and He desires for all mankind to be with Him for eternity.

- Heaven and hell are real.

- Jesus desires that we move beyond the initial stage of relationship and capture His heart, a heart that wants everyone to come to know Him and partake of His inheritance.

Questions to Consider

1. How often do you spend quality time with the Lord?

2. Are those around you aware of what the Bible says?

3. What is your view of hell? Describe.

4. What are you doing to prevent those around you from being separated for eternity from God?

5. Are you aware of the different weapons God has made available to you?

6. Have you made the decision to accept His free gift of salvation?

7. Are those around you aware of the free gift of salvation? Explain.

8. Do you want to spend eternity with Jesus?

9. Do you have complete trust in God's abilities? Explain.

10. Where are you in your relationship with Jesus? Describe.

11. What are you doing to support God's kingdom?

Epilogue

I would like somehow to think I have reached a point in my relationship with Jesus where I can slow down. But in reality there are no "rest areas" in our journey toward developing an intimate relationship with Jesus.

The last decade of my life has brought a great awakening and understanding of the things of God. I have come to know a great Person, the Holy Spirit. He is a divine Person whose goal is that we come to know Jesus. Thanks to Him, the Bible has become a great source of the revelations of Jesus Christ.

I have come to realize that in order to know Jesus we must first understand the Bible. Also, only with the help of the Holy Spirit can we really begin to know Jesus and receive the spirit of revelation to understand the Bible.

We can spend our whole life trying to develop a relationship with Jesus. But without the assistance of the Holy Spirit our approach will always lead to frustration and loneliness.

Not until the Holy Spirit takes us by the hand and brings us closer to Jesus can we start to develop an intimate relationship with Him.

I hope this book will help you in your search for intimacy with Jesus. I have learned that the Bible is true and that God desires to spend time with us and to share His intimacy with us. He is not looking for special people; He is just looking for someone who is willing to listen and obey Him.

> For the LORD detests a perverse man but takes the upright into his confidence.
>
> —PROVERBS 3:32

> The Lord confides in those who fear him; he makes his covenant known to them.
>
> —PSALM 25:14

Our time on this earth should not restrain us from developing an intimate relationship with Jesus. On the contrary, it should encourage us to reach out to Him. Eternity with Him is a "long time" but we can start here. Now is the time to engage in an intimate relationship with the Savior so when the time comes to be with Him we will not be strangers, but friends.

As we continue our search for an understanding of and relationship with God, consider Jesus' words:

> Greater love has no one than this, that he lay down his life for his friends. You are my friends if you do what I command. I no longer call you servants, because a servant does not know his master's business. Instead, I have called you friends, for everything that I learned from my father I have made known to you.
>
> —JOHN 15:13–15

These scriptures speak of the sacrifice God made by sending His only Son, Jesus, to die for us, to restore the intimacy we once had with Him in the Garden of Eden. It is a reminder that God desires to engage in an intimate relationship with us.

As I continue to develop a deeper relationship with the Holy Spirit, the reality of Jesus and the things of God have become more clear and attainable to me. I still have a long road ahead of me as a believer, but I have made a commitment not to allow my fears to deprive me of developing a closer relationship with God. He is all the Bible claims He is—and so much more. He is the God that I know.

He offers us salvation—for free. However, our relationship with Him depends on how much we invest in our spiritual growth.

After several years of spending intimate moments with the Holy Spirit, I realize that I have just scratched the surface of our relationship.

> "Do not let your hearts be troubled, trust in God, trust also in me. In my father's house are many rooms; if it were not so, I would have told you, I am going there to prepare a place for you. And if I go and prepare a place for you, I will come back and take you to be with me that you also may be where I am. You know the way to the place where I am going." Thomas said to him, "Lord, we don't know where you are going, so how can we know the way?" Jesus answered, "I am the way and the truth and the life. No one comes to the Father except through me."
> —JOHN 14:11–27

I would like to extend an invitation to you. If you have not accepted Jesus into your heart, please pray the following prayer:

Lord Jesus, I recognize that you are the Son of God and that the only way to the Father is through You. Please forgive my sins and come into my heart. Help me to be like You. Amen.

If you have already accepted Jesus into your heart, I encourage you to continue your journey of developing an intimate relationship with Jesus and to share this book with your family, friends, and neighbors. And never forget that it is through faith in Christ's power that we will be saved:

> To Him who is able to keep you from falling and to present you before his glorious presence without fault and with great joy—to the only God our Savior be glory, majesty, power, and authority, through Jesus Christ our Lord, before all ages, now and forevermore! Amen.
>
> —JUDE 1: 24